christmas at home

NO-BAKE
Holiday
RECIPES

AMY ROBERTSON

BARBOUR
PUBLISHING

© 2003 by Barbour Publishing, Inc.

ISBN 1-59310-042-6

Cover image © PhotoDisc

Scripture quotations are taken from the King James Version of the Bible.

Published by Barbour Publishing, Inc., P.O. Box 719, Uhrichsville, Ohio 44683, www.barbourbooks.com

 Member of the
Evangelical Christian
Publishers Association

Printed in Canada.
5 4 3 2 1

contents

Therefore the Lord himself shall give you a sign;
Behold, a virgin shall conceive, and bear a son,
and shall call his name Immanuel.

ISAIAH 7:14

cakes & pies

For unto us a child is born, unto us a son is given:
and the government shall be upon his shoulder:
and his name shall be called Wonderful, Counsellor,
The mighty God, The everlasting Father, The Prince of Peace.

ISAIAH 9:6

Crunchy ICE CREAM CAKE

4 cups toasted rice cereal
    squares, crumbled
$\frac{1}{3}$ cup brown sugar
6 tablespoons butter, melted
1 (3.9-ounce) package instant
    butterscotch pudding mix

$\frac{1}{2}$ cup chunky peanut butter
$1\frac{2}{3}$ cups milk
1 quart vanilla ice cream, softened
$\frac{1}{2}$ cup chopped peanuts

Grease a 9-inch square baking pan; set aside. In a large bowl, combine crumbled cereal, brown sugar, and butter; mix well. Measure ¼ cup of the cereal mixture and set aside. Pat remaining cereal mixture firmly into the bottom of prepared pan. Refrigerate for about 1 hour or until firm. Using an electric mixer, combine butterscotch pudding mix, peanut butter, and milk on low speed until well blended; fold in vanilla ice cream and mix well. Pour ice cream mixture into prepared pan; sprinkle with reserved crumb mixture; then sprinkle with peanuts. Cover with aluminum foil and freeze at least 6 hours.

Chocolate CHEESECAKE

½ cup butter or margarine, melted
1½ cups graham cracker crumbs
½ cup sugar
⅔ cup water
1 envelope gelatin, unflavored
2 (8-ounce) packages cream cheese, softened

4 (1-ounce) squares semisweet chocolate, melted
1 (14-ounce) can sweetened condensed milk
1 teaspoon vanilla extract
1 cup whipped cream

In a 9-inch springform pan, mix together the butter, graham cracker crumbs, and sugar. Press firmly against the bottom of the pan (do not line the sides). In a small saucepan, add $2/3$ cup water. Sprinkle the gelatin over the water and let stand for 1 minute. Over low heat, stir the gelatin until it dissolves; set aside. In a large bowl, beat the cream cheese and chocolate until fluffy. Gradually beat in the sweetened condensed milk. Add the vanilla and beat until smooth. Stir the gelatin mixture into the cream cheese mixture. Fold in the whipped cream. Pour the mixture into the prepared pan. Chill in the refrigerator for 3 hours or until set. Garnish with whipped cream. Keep refrigerated.

CHOCOLATE  CHEESECAKE

1 (7-ounce) package caramels
¼ cup evaporated milk
¾ cup chopped pecans, divided
1 (9-inch) prepared chocolate
    crumb piecrust
2 (3-ounce) packages cream cheese,
    softened

½ cup sour cream
1¼ cups milk
1 (3.9-ounce) package instant
    chocolate pudding mix
½ cup fudge topping

Place caramels and evaporated milk in a large saucepan. Mix over medium heat, stirring constantly until smooth. Stir in ½ cup chopped pecans. Pour into the piecrust. Combine cream cheese, sour cream, milk, and pudding mix in a blender. Process until smooth. Pour pudding mixture over caramel layer, covering evenly. Loosely cover pie and chill until set. Drizzle fudge topping over pudding layer in a decorative pattern. Sprinkle top of cake with remaining pecans. Loosely cover and chill in refrigerator.

FROZEN *Peppermint* CHEESECAKE

1 (8-ounce) package cream
   cheese, softened
1 (14-ounce) can sweetened
   condensed milk
1 cup hard peppermint candy,
   crushed

Red food coloring
2 cups frozen whipped topping,
   thawed
2 (9-inch) prepared chocolate
   crumb piecrusts

Place cream cheese in a large bowl. With an electric mixer on low speed, beat until fluffy. Gradually beat in sweetened condensed milk. Stir in crushed peppermint candy and food coloring. Fold in whipped topping. Pour into piecrusts and cover. Freeze 6 hours or until firm. Garnish with peppermint candies.

Pretzel CHEESECAKE

1 cup pretzel crumbs
1/4 cup butter, melted
1/2 cup sugar
1 container frozen whipped topping, thawed

1 (3-ounce) package cream cheese, softened
1/2 cup powdered sugar
1 (21-ounce) can cherry pie filling

In a 9-inch pie pan, combine pretzel crumbs, butter, and sugar. Press into bottom of pan to form a crust; set aside. Combine whipped topping, cream cheese, and powdered sugar in a medium bowl; beat well. Spread filling over prepared crust. Top with cherry pie filling. Chill in refrigerator for at least 2 hours before serving.

STRABERRY *Angel Food* CAKE

1 small box strawberry-flavored gelatin
1 cup hot water
$\frac{1}{2}$ cup ice water
2 cups whipped topping, thawed
2 small cans frozen strawberries,
    drained

1 angel food cake
1 cup berry juice
1 tablespoon butter
1 tablespoon cornstarch

In a large bowl, combine gelatin, hot water, and ice water. Chill until slightly firm. Beat until stiff. Add whipped topping and drained strawberries. Break cake into pieces. Layer cake and gelatin mixture in 9x13-inch pan. End with cake on top. In a small saucepan, cook juice, butter, and cornstarch until clear. Cool. Drizzle over top of cake. Keep refrigerated.

No-Bake FRUITCAKE

1 cup pecans, chopped
1 cup raisins, chopped
1 cup walnuts, chopped
1 (4-ounce) jar maraschino cherries,
   drained and chopped

1 (14-ounce) can sweetened
   condensed milk
1 (12-ounce) package
   vanilla wafers, crushed

In a medium bowl, combine the pecans, raisins, walnuts, cherries, sweetened condensed milk, and vanilla wafers. The dough will be thick; use your hands to get it completely mixed. Shape the dough into a ring on top of a dinner plate. Wrap the cake and plate in many layers of plastic wrap. Refrigerate the cake for at least a week to allow the flavors to blend and all of the milk to be absorbed.

VERY *Berry* PIE

1 cup water
¾ cup sugar
2 tablespoons cornstarch
3 tablespoons raspberry-flavored gelatin
3¼ cups sliced strawberries

1 cup blueberries
1 cup raspberries
1 (9-inch) ready-to-use
   shortbread piecrust
Whipped topping (optional)

In a medium saucepan, over medium heat, combine water, sugar, and cornstarch. Bring to a boil, stirring constantly. Boil and stir for 1 minute; remove from heat. Add gelatin and stir until dissolved. Refrigerate about 30 minutes, stirring occasionally, until mixture thickens. Stir the berries into the gelatin mixture. Pour into the prepared crust. Refrigerate about 2 hours or until set. Top with whipped cream if desired. Store covered in the refrigerator.

Chocolate PIE

3 (1-ounce) squares semisweet
    chocolate
1 (14-ounce) can sweetened
    condensed milk
$\frac{1}{4}$ teaspoon salt
$\frac{1}{4}$ cup hot water

2 egg yolks
1 teaspoon vanilla extract
1 cup whipped cream
1 (9-inch) prepared pie shell
Additional whipped cream
Chocolate shavings

In a large saucepan, combine chocolate, sweetened condensed milk, and salt. Cook over medium heat until thick and bubbly, stirring constantly. Add water and egg yolks, stirring quickly until the mixture is thick and bubbly again. Remove from heat and stir in the vanilla. Allow to cool for 15 minutes. Chill in the refrigerator for an additional 20–30 minutes; stir. Fold the whipped cream into the cooled chocolate mixture; stir. Pour the chocolate mixture into the prepared pie shell. Chill for $2\frac{1}{2}$–3 hours, or until chocolate is set. Top with the additional whipped cream. Garnish with chocolate shavings. Keep refrigerated.

CREAMY *Lime* PIE

1 (14-ounce) can sweetened
   condensed milk
½ cup lime juice (from concentrate)
Green food coloring

1 cup whipped cream
1 (9-inch) prepared graham
   cracker piecrust
Whipped cream (optional)
Lime slices (optional)

In a large bowl, combine sweetened condensed milk, lime juice, and green food coloring; stir well. Fold in the whipped cream. Pour the mixture into the prepared piecrust. Chill pie in the refrigerator for 3 hours or until filling is set. Garnish with whipped cream and lime slices if desired. Keep refrigerated.

Pink Lemonade PIE

1 quart vanilla ice cream, softened
½ (12-ounce) can frozen pink
    lemonade concentrate, thawed
1 (4-ounce) container frozen
    whipped topping, thawed

Red food coloring
1 (9-inch) prepared graham
    cracker crust
Lime peel (optional)

In a large bowl, combine ice cream, lemonade, whipped topping, and 4–5 drops of food coloring; mix well. Pour filling into prepared piecrust. Freeze for 4 hours or until filling is firm. Let stand at room temperature for 5–10 minutes before cutting. Garnish with lime peel.

Grasshopper PIE

1 (8-ounce) package cream cheese,
softened
1 (14-ounce) can sweetened
condensed milk
Green food coloring

16 chocolate mint cookies,
crushed
1 (8-ounce) container frozen
whipped topping, thawed
1 (9-inch) prepared chocolate
crumb piecrust

Place cream cheese in a large bowl. Beat with an electric mixer, on low speed, until fluffy. Gradually beat in the sweetened condensed milk until smooth. Add the food coloring; stir. Stir in the crushed cookies, saving some for garnish. Fold in the whipped topping. Pour the mixture into the prepared piecrust. Chill in the refrigerator for 3 hours or until filling is set. Garnish with cookie pieces. Keep refrigerated.

BLACK *Forest* PIE

4 (1-ounce) baking chocolate squares, broken into pieces
1 (14-ounce) can sweetened condensed milk
1 teaspoon almond extract

1½ cups frozen whipped topping, thawed
1 (9-inch) prepared piecrust
1 (21-ounce) can cherry pie filling, chilled

In a large saucepan, combine chocolate pieces and sweetened condensed milk. Cook over medium heat, stirring constantly, until chocolate is melted and smooth. Remove from heat and stir in almond extract. Pour mixture into a large bowl and allow to cool completely in the refrigerator. Beat cooled mixture until smooth. Fold the whipped topping into the chocolate mixture. Pour into the prepared piecrust. Refrigerate 4–5 hours or until set. Before serving, pour cherry pie filling over pie. Refrigerate leftover pie.

Banana Split PIE

1 (3.9-ounce) package instant vanilla
  pudding mix
1¼ cups cold milk
1 (12-ounce) container frozen whipped
  topping, thawed and divided
2 bananas, sliced into ¼-inch slices

1 (9-inch) prepared chocolate
  crumb crust
1 (12-ounce) jar hot fudge topping
1 (20-ounce) can pineapple chunks,
  drained
12 maraschino cherries with stems,
  drained
3 tablespoons walnut pieces

In a large bowl, stir together pudding mix and milk. Beat until smooth and thick. Fold in 2 cups of the whipped topping and 1 sliced banana. Reserve ½ of the banana pudding mixture and spread the remainder into the piecrust. Reserve 3 tablespoons of the hot fudge topping for drizzling on top. Gently spread ½ of the remaining hot fudge topping over the banana pudding in the piecrust. Repeat layers with the remaining banana pudding and fudge topping. Refrigerate 1 hour or until firm. Arrange the pineapple chunks in a single layer on top of the pie. Spread with the remaining whipped topping, swirling topping into peaks with the back of a spoon. Refrigerate for 30 minutes. Heat the reserved fudge topping in the microwave until hot enough to pour. Drizzle the topping over top of the pie with a fork. Garnish with maraschino cherries and walnut pieces.

Cherry CHEESE PIE

1 (8-ounce) package cream cheese,
    softened
½ cup sugar
2 cups frozen whipped topping,
    thawed

1 (9-inch) prepared graham cracker
    crust
1 (21-ounce) can cherry pie
    filling

In a medium bowl, beat together cream cheese and sugar until fluffy. Fold in whipped topping and stir until the mixture is smooth. Pour into the prepared graham cracker crust. Cover and refrigerate for 3 hours. Spoon the cherry pie filling over top of the pie. Keep refrigerated.

Chocolate PEANUT BUTTER PIE

2 (3.9-ounce) packages single-serve, ready-made chocolate pudding

⅓ cup peanut butter

1 (8-ounce) container frozen whipped topping, thawed

1 (9-inch) prepared graham cracker crust

In a large bowl, combine the pudding and peanut butter. Stir until mixture is smooth. Fold in the whipped topping and mix until well blended. Pour the mixture into the prepared piecrust. Put pie in freezer until firm. Partially thaw in the refrigerator for about 2 hours before serving. Store in the freezer and thaw as needed.

Cookies and Cream PIE

1 (3.9-ounce) package instant
chocolate pudding mix
1 (8-ounce) container frozen
whipped topping, thawed

1½ cups chocolate sandwich cookies,
crushed
1 (9-inch) prepared chocolate
crumb piecrust

Prepare the pudding as directed on the package for pie filling; allow to set. When the pudding is ready, fold in the whipped topping. Add the crushed cookies; stir. Pour mixture into the prepared piecrust. Freeze pie until firm. Thaw in the refrigerator before serving.

No-Bake PUMPKIN PIE

4 ounces cream cheese, softened
1 tablespoon milk
1 tablespoon sugar
1½ cups frozen whipped
    topping, thawed
1 (9-inch) prepared graham
    cracker piecrust
1 cup cold milk

2 (3.9-ounce) packages instant
    vanilla pudding mix
1 (15-ounce) can pumpkin puree
1 teaspoon ground cinnamon
½ teaspoon ground ginger
¼ teaspoon ground cloves
Additional whipped topping,
    thawed

In a large bowl, whisk together the cream cheese, milk, and sugar until mixture is smooth. Fold in the whipped topping; stir well. Spread mixture onto the bottom of prepared crust. In a large bowl, combine milk, pudding mix, pumpkin, cinnamon, ginger, and cloves; mix well. When the pudding mixture is thick, spread it over the cream cheese layer. Refrigerate for 4 hours or until set. Garnish with whipped topping. Keep refrigerated.

Butterscotch PUDDING PIE

2 (3.9-ounce) packages instant
   butterscotch pudding mix
2¾ cups cold milk

1 (9-inch) prepared pie shell
1 cup frozen whipped topping,
   thawed

In a large bowl, combine the pudding mix and milk. Beat with a wire whisk for 2½ minutes. Pour pudding into the prepared pie shell. Refrigerate for at least 1 hour or until the filling is set. Spoon whipped topping around the crust. Garnish the pie with holiday sprinkles scattered over the whipped topping. Keep refrigerated.

Avocado PIE

2 avocados, peeled, pitted, and pureed
½ cup lemon juice
1 (5-ounce) can sweetened
   condensed milk
1 (9-inch) prepared graham cracker
   piecrust

Whipped topping (optional)
Lemon peel (optional)

In a medium bowl, combine the avocados, lemon juice, and sweetened condensed milk; mix well. Pour mixture into the prepared crust. Refrigerate for 2–3 hours before serving. Garnish with whipped topping and lemon peel if desired.

And so it was, that, while they were there,

the days were accomplished that she should be delivered.

And she brought forth her firstborn son,

and wrapped him in swaddling clothes,

and laid him in a manger;

because there was no room for them in the inn.

LUKE 2:6–7

cookies

And suddenly there was with the angel
a multitude of the heavenly host praising God, and saying,
Glory to God in the highest,
and on earth peace, good will toward men.

LUKE 2:13–14

NO-BAKE *Fudge* COOKIES

½ cup (1 stick) butter or margarine,
    cut into pieces
½ cup milk
2 cups sugar
⅓ cup cocoa powder

1 teaspoon salt
1 teaspoon vanilla extract
4 cups quick-cooking oats
Butterscotch fudge cutouts (optional,
    see page 40 for recipe)

Line a tray or cookie sheet with waxed paper. Combine butter and milk in a large microwave-safe bowl. Microwave on high (100%) for 1 minute or until butter is melted. Stir in the sugar and cocoa until mixed. Microwave on high for 1½ minutes; stir. Microwave on high an additional 1½–3 minutes or until sugar is completely dissolved. Stir in salt, vanilla, and oats. Drop by spoonfuls onto prepared tray or cookie sheet. Flatten slightly and let stand until firm. Top with butterscotch fudge cutouts if desired. Makes 3 dozen.

Butterscotch Fudge CUTOUTS

3 ⅓ cups butterscotch chips

1 (14-ounce) can sweetened
condensed milk

Line a 15x10x1-inch jelly-roll pan with aluminum foil. Combine butter-scotch chips and sweetened condensed milk in a large, microwave-safe bowl. Microwave on high (100%) for 1 minute. Continue heating for 15–20 seconds at a time, until the chips are melted and the mixture is smooth when stirred. Immediately spread into prepared pan. Cover, and refrigerate until fudge is firm. Use the edges of the foil to lift fudge out of the pan. Peel off the foil and place fudge on a cutting board. Using small cookie cutters, cut fudge into shapes. Makes about 2 pounds.

Christmas WREATHS

½ cup butter
30 large marshmallows
1 ½ teaspoons green food coloring

1 teaspoon vanilla extract
4 cups cornflakes cereal
2 tablespoons cinnamon candies

Melt the butter in a large saucepan over low heat. Add the marshmallows, and heat until completely melted, stirring constantly. Remove from heat, and add the food coloring, vanilla, and cornflakes. With lightly greased fingers, quickly drop spoonfuls of the mixture onto waxed paper, and form it into the shape of a wreath. Immediately decorate with the cinnamon candies. Allow to cool at room temperature before removing from waxed paper. Store in an airtight container.

Cathedral WINDOWS

¼ cup butter
2 cups semisweet chocolate chips
2 eggs, beaten
1 cup chopped pecans

1 (10½-ounce) package colored
   miniature marshmallows
⅓ cup powdered sugar
   for decoration

Line a 9x5-inch loaf pan with foil; set aside. Place butter and chocolate chips in a microwave-safe bowl. Microwave until melted, stirring frequently. Stir in the eggs, pecans, and colored marshmallows. Pour the mixture into the prepared pan. Dust with powdered sugar and refrigerate until firm. Remove chilled dough from loaf pan, gently peel off the foil, and slice into ¼-inch slices.

Butterscotch DROPS

1²⁄₃ cups butterscotch chips   5½ cups cornflakes cereal
1 cup creamy peanut butter

Line two baking sheets with waxed paper. Place the butterscotch chips in a microwave-safe bowl. Microwave on medium-high (70%) for 1 minute; stir. Microwave at additional 10-second intervals until melted and smooth. Stir in the peanut butter until smooth. Add the cornflakes and mix until evenly coated. Drop mixture by rounded spoonfuls onto the prepared baking sheets. Refrigerate for 20 minutes or until firm. Store in an airtight container in the refrigerator.

Peanut Butter COOKIES

1 cup light corn syrup	1½ cups creamy peanut butter
1 cup sugar	6 cups cornflakes cereal

In a medium saucepan, over medium heat, combine the corn syrup and sugar. Bring the mixture to a boil. Reduce heat, and stir until the sugar has dissolved. Add the peanut butter and stir until thoroughly combined. Remove from heat. Pour the cornflakes into a large mixing bowl. Pour the peanut butter mixture over the cereal and toss until coated. Drop by rounded teaspoonfuls onto waxed paper. Cool at room temperature until firm.

NO-BAKE *Chocolate Oat* BARS

1 cup butter
½ cup brown sugar, packed
1 teaspoon vanilla extract

3 cups quick-cooking oats
1 cup semisweet chocolate
   chips
½ cup peanut butter

Lightly grease a 9-inch square pan; set aside. In a large saucepan, over medium heat, melt the butter. Stir in the brown sugar and vanilla. Mix in the oats. Cook over low heat for 2–3 minutes. Press half of the mixture into the bottom of the prepared pan. Reserve the other half for topping. Melt chocolate chips and peanut butter in the microwave until smooth. Pour the melted chocolate mixture over the layer in the pan, and spread evenly with the back of a spoon. Crumble the remaining oat mixture over the chocolate layer, pressing gently. Cover, and refrigerate overnight. Bring to room temperature before cutting into bars.

Traditional NO-BAKE COOKIES

½ cup (1 stick) butter or margarine
½ cup milk
2 cups sugar
½ cup cocoa powder

1 cup peanut butter
1 teaspoon vanilla
3 cups oats

Combine butter, milk, sugar, and cocoa powder in a large saucepan. Bring to a rolling boil. Boil for 3 minutes (do not overboil), and add peanut butter, vanilla, and oats. Drop by heaping teaspoonfuls onto a sheet of waxed paper. Let cool until firm. Store in an airtight container in a cool, dry place.

Oatmeal MACAROONS

½ cup shortening
½ cup milk
2 cups sugar

½ cup cocoa powder
½ cup flaked coconut
3 cups oats

In a medium saucepan, over medium heat, combine the shortening, milk, and sugar. Bring the mixture to a boil, stirring constantly. Boil for 2 minutes. Remove from heat and stir in cocoa, coconut, and oats; mix well. Drop the mixture by spoonfuls onto waxed paper. Allow to cool for 2–3 hours. Store in an airtight container.

Granola BITES

1 cup powdered sugar
1 cup creamy peanut butter
⅓ cup milk
1 teaspoon vanilla extract

1 ½ cups oats
1 cup granola cereal
1 ¾ cups (11-ounce package)
   peanut butter and milk
   chocolate chips

Line two baking sheets with waxed paper. In a large bowl, combine powdered sugar, peanut butter, milk, and vanilla; mix well. Stir in the oats, cereal, and chips. Mix until the cereal is evenly coated. Roll the mixture into 1-inch balls and place on the prepared baking sheets. Let stand until firm. Store in an airtight container.

MARSHMALLOW *No-Bake* COOKIES

1 cup sugar
1 cup light corn syrup
4 cups cornflakes cereal

12 ounces creamy peanut butter
1 cup semisweet chocolate chips
1 cup miniature marshmallows

In a large saucepan, combine the sugar and light corn syrup; cook over low heat until the sugar is dissolved. Remove from heat. Stir in the cornflakes and peanut butter. Fold in chocolate chips and marshmallows. Stir until thoroughly mixed. Drop by rounded teaspoonfuls onto waxed paper and allow to cool until firm. Store in an airtight container.

Peanut Butter NO-BAKE COOKIES

2 cups sugar
$^3/_4$ cup butter
$^3/_4$ cup milk

$^1/_2$ teaspoon vanilla extract
$1^1/_2$ cups peanut butter
$4^1/_2$ cups quick-cooking oats

In a medium saucepan, over medium heat, combine the sugar, butter, and milk. Bring to a rolling boil and boil for 1 full minute. Remove from heat and stir in the vanilla and peanut butter. Mix in the oats and stir until the mixture begins to cool. Drop the mixture by spoonfuls onto a sheet of waxed paper. Allow to cool until set.

No-Bake PUDDING COOKIES

2 cups sugar
¾ cup butter
½ (12-ounce) can evaporated milk

1 (3.9-ounce) package instant
    butterscotch pudding mix
3½ cups quick-cooking oats

In a medium saucepan, combine the sugar, butter, and evaporated milk. Bring to a boil and allow to boil for 1 minute. Remove from heat and stir in the instant pudding and oatmeal. Spoon the mixture onto a sheet of waxed paper. Allow to cool until firm.

Chocolate DATE COOKIES

1 pound graham cracker crumbs
1 (16-ounce) container chocolate frosting

2 tablespoons butter, melted
4 ounces pitted dates, coarsely chopped
$\frac{1}{4}$ cup powdered sugar

In a large bowl, combine graham cracker crumbs, frosting, melted butter, and dates; mix well. Form the mixture into 1-inch balls and roll in the powdered sugar. Store in an airtight container.

Stovetop COOKIES

1 cup flaked coconut
1 cup sugar
2 large eggs, beaten
1 cup chopped dates

1 tablespoon butter
2 cups crisp rice cereal
1 cup chopped pecans
1 teaspoon vanilla extract

Sprinkle the coconut evenly onto a 15x10x1-inch pan lined with waxed paper. Set aside. In a large saucepan, combine the sugar and eggs; stir well. Add the dates and butter. Cook over low heat, stirring constantly, for 8 minutes or until the mixture is thick and bubbly. Remove from heat, and stir in the cereal, pecans, and vanilla; mix well. Spread the cereal mixture evenly onto the prepared pan. Let stand for 15 minutes. Roll the mixture into a 15-inch log. Allow to cool completely. Cut into ½-inch-thick slices. Store in an airtight container.

Shoestring POTATO COOKIES

1 (12-ounce) package
  butterscotch chips
3 tablespoons creamy peanut butter

4 ounces shoestring potatoes
1 cup raisins

Melt the butterscotch chips and peanut butter in a medium saucepan over low heat. Place the shoestring potatoes in a large mixing bowl. Pour the melted butterscotch chip mixture over the shoestring potatoes. Stir in the raisins. Mix until well combined. Drop by teaspoonfuls onto waxed paper. Chill in the refrigerator until firm.

Fruity CEREAL COOKIES

1 (12-ounce) package
white chocolate chips
2 cups sweetened rice and
corn cereal squares

1 cup dried fruit (cranberries,
cherries, raisins)
¼ cup peanuts

In a large microwave-safe bowl, microwave white chocolate chips on high (100%) at 30-second intervals until completely melted, stirring between intervals. Gently stir in cereal squares, fruit, and peanuts. Stir until well coated. Drop clusters onto a sheet of waxed paper with a tablespoon. Refrigerate for 1 hour. Store in an airtight container in a cool, dry place.

Snowballs

2 1/4 cups chocolate sandwich
  cookie crumbs
1 cup pecans, finely chopped
1 1/2 cups powdered sugar,
  sifted and divided

1/3 cup coconut flakes
1/4 cup light corn syrup
1/4 cup strawberry preserves

In a large bowl, combine cookie crumbs, pecans, 1/4 cup powdered sugar, and coconut; mix well. Stir in the corn syrup and preserves. Shape the mixture into 1-inch balls. Roll each ball in the remaining powdered sugar. Store in an airtight container.

Orange FINGERS

3 ½ cups vanilla wafer crumbs
1 (16-ounce) box powdered
  sugar, sifted
1 ½ cups chopped pecans

1 (6-ounce) can frozen orange juice
  concentrate, thawed
½ cup butter, melted
1 (7-ounce) package flaked coconut

In a large bowl, combine vanilla wafer crumbs, powdered sugar, and pecans; mix well. Stir in the orange juice and butter. Shape into 2-inch rolls. Roll each piece in the flaked coconut. Refrigerate overnight.

Coconut BONBONS

¼ cup butter
1 pound powdered sugar
1 cup sweetened condensed milk
2 cups flaked coconut

9 (1-ounce) squares
    semisweet chocolate
2 tablespoons shortening

In a medium bowl, combine butter, powdered sugar, and sweetened condensed milk. Stir in the coconut; mix well. Roll the mixture into 1-inch balls. Refrigerate until set, about 1 hour. Melt chocolate and shortening over a double boiler, stirring occasionally until melted and smooth. Remove from heat and stir. Use toothpicks to hold the balls while dipping in the chocolate. Set on waxed paper to dry.

For God so loved the world,
that he gave his only begotten Son,
that whosoever believeth in him should not perish,
but have everlasting life.

JOHN 3:16

candy & fudge

And she shall bring forth a son, and thou shalt call his name JESUS:

for he shall save his people from their sins.

MATTHEW 1:21

THE HISTORY OF THE *Candy Cane*

The candy cane, seen mostly during the holiday season, stands as an important Christmas symbol. A candy maker wanted to create a way to express the meaning of Christmas through the imagination of candy. That is when he came up with the idea of the candy cane. There are several different symbols incorporated into the candy cane. First, he used a plain white peppermint stick. The color white symbolizes the purity and sinless nature of Jesus. He then decided to add three red stripes to symbolize the pain inflicted upon Jesus before His death on the cross and a bold stripe to represent the blood He shed for mankind. He made it in the shape of a cane, so when looked at, it looks like a shepherd's staff, which represents that Jesus is the Shepherd of man. If you turn the cane upside down, you will notice the shape of the letter "J" symbolizing the first letter in Jesus' name. The candy cane serves as a lasting reminder of what Christmas is really all about.

Chow Mein CANDIES

2 (6-ounce) packages
    semisweet chocolate chips
2 (6-ounce) packages
    butterscotch chips

2 (3-ounce) cans chow mein noodles
1/2 cup cashews

In a large saucepan, combine chocolate chips and butterscotch chips. Melt over low heat, stirring constantly, until smooth. Remove from heat and stir in the noodles and cashews. Drop by teaspoonfuls onto a sheet of waxed paper and let cool until set. Store in an airtight container.

Chocolate-Covered CHERRIES

2½ cups sugar
¼ cup margarine
1 tablespoon milk
½ teaspoon almond extract

4 (4-ounce) jars maraschino
  cherries with stems, drained
2 cups semisweet chocolate chips
2 tablespoons shortening

In a medium bowl, combine sugar, margarine, milk, and almond extract; stir. On a lightly floured surface, knead the mixture into a large ball. Roll into 1-inch individual balls. Flatten the balls into 2-inch circles. Leaving the stems sticking out, wrap the cherries in the circles by lightly rolling in hands. Place the wrapped cherries on a sheet of waxed paper and chill in the refrigerator for at least 4 hours. In a medium saucepan over medium heat, melt the chocolate chips and shortening. Holding the balls by the stem of the cherry sticking out, dip the chilled cherries into the chocolate mixture. Chill in the refrigerator.

Chocolate Caramel CANDY

1 cup milk chocolate chips
¼ cup butterscotch chips
¼ cup creamy peanut butter
¼ cup butter
1 cup sugar
¼ cup evaporated milk
1½ cups marshmallow crème
¼ cup creamy peanut butter

1 teaspoon vanilla extract
1½ cups chopped salted peanuts
14 ounces individually wrapped
    caramels, unwrapped
¼ cup heavy cream
¼ cup butterscotch chips
¼ cup creamy peanut butter
1 cup milk chocolate chips

Grease a 9x13-inch pan. Combine the chocolate chips, butterscotch chips, and peanut butter in a small saucepan. Cook over low heat, stirring constantly, until melted and smooth. Spread onto the bottom of the prepared pan. Refrigerate until set. In a heavy saucepan, melt the butter over medium heat. Stir in the sugar and evaporated milk. Bring the mixture to a boil and cook for 5 minutes, stirring constantly. Remove from heat and stir in the marshmallow crème, $1/4$ cup of peanut butter, and the vanilla. Add the peanuts and spread mixture over the cooled layer. Refrigerate until set. Combine the caramels and cream in a saucepan. Cook over low heat until melted, stirring constantly. Spread over the refrigerated layers. Refrigerate until set. In another saucepan, combine the last three ingredients. Cook over low heat, stirring constantly, until melted and smooth. Pour the mixture over the refrigerated caramel layer. Refrigerate for at least 1 hour. Cut into 1-inch squares. Store in the refrigerator.

Buckeyes

1 cup powdered sugar
½ cup creamy peanut butter

3 tablespoons butter or margarine
1 pound milk chocolate

In a large mixing bowl, stir together powdered sugar, peanut butter, and butter until well combined. Shape into about 30 1-inch balls. Place balls on a baking sheet lined with waxed paper. Let stand for about 25 minutes or until dry. Place water in the bottom of a double boiler to within ½-inch of upper pan. Make sure the upper pan does not touch the water. While balls are cooling and water is heating, finely chop the chocolate so it will melt quickly. Bring the water to a boil. Remove from heat and place about ¼ of the chocolate in the top of the double boiler. Stir until melted. Add about ½ cup more, stir, and repeat until all chocolate is melted. Stir until chocolate reaches 120 degrees; reheat if necessary to reach this temperature. After chocolate has reached 120 degrees, refill bottom of the double boiler with cool water to within ½ inch of upper pan. Stir frequently until chocolate cools to 83 degrees. This should take about 30 minutes. Using a toothpick, dip balls in chocolate, working quickly and stirring chocolate frequently to keep it evenly heated. Place balls on cookie sheet. (Chocolate will stay close to 83 degrees for about 30 minutes. If temperature falls below 80 degrees, chocolate must be remelted.) Store tightly covered in a cool, dry place.

Chocolate PEANUT CLUSTERS

2 tablespoons creamy peanut butter
1 (6-ounce) package semisweet
   chocolate chips

1 (6-ounce) package
   butterscotch chips
2 cups salted peanuts

In a medium saucepan, add peanut butter, chocolate chips, and butterscotch chips. Cook over medium heat until chips are melted and smooth. Remove from heat and add peanuts. Drop by rounded spoonfuls onto waxed paper.

Easy Microwave PEANUT BRITTLE

1 cup sugar
½ cup light corn syrup
1 dash salt
1 cup shelled raw peanuts

1 tablespoon butter or margarine
1 teaspoon vanilla
1½ teaspoons baking soda

Grease a cookie sheet generously. Combine sugar, corn syrup, and salt in a 3-quart casserole dish; stir in the peanuts. Microwave on high (100%) for 8–10 minutes or until light brown. Stir in the remaining ingredients until the mixture is light and foamy. Quickly spread the mixture as thinly as possible on the prepared cookie sheet.

Chocolate TRUFFLES

6 ounces semisweet baking chocolate, chopped
2 tablespoons butter
¼ cup heavy whipping cream

1 tablespoon shortening
1 cup milk chocolate chips
Finely chopped nuts, shaved coconut, decorating candies (optional)

Line a cookie sheet with aluminum foil; set aside. In a medium saucepan, over low heat, melt baking chocolate, stirring constantly. Remove from heat. Stir in butter until completely melted. Add the whipping cream; stir. Refrigerate for 15–20 minutes, stirring frequently, until mixture is thick enough to hold shape. Drop the mixture by teaspoonfuls onto the prepared cookie sheet. Shape each one into a 1-inch ball. Freeze balls for 30 minutes. Heat the shortening and chocolate chips in a saucepan over low heat, stirring constantly, until the mixture is smooth; remove from heat. Dip each ball into the melted chocolate mixture. Place on foil-covered cookie sheet. Sprinkle chopped nuts, coconut, or decorating candies if desired. Refrigerate truffles for 10–15 minutes or until the coating is set. Serve at room temperature. Store in an airtight container in a cool, dry place.

Chocolate-Covered ORANGE BALLS

1 pound powdered sugar
1 (12-ounce) package vanilla
   wafers, crushed
1 cup chopped walnuts

¼ pound butter
1 (6-ounce) can frozen orange juice
   concentrate, thawed
1½ pounds milk chocolate chips,
   melted

In a large bowl, combine the powdered sugar, vanilla wafers, walnuts, butter, and orange juice. Mix well and shape into 1-inch balls. Place balls on a sheet of waxed paper and allow to dry for 1 hour. Place chocolate chips in the top of a double boiler. Stir frequently over medium heat until melted. Dip balls into the melted chocolate and place in decorative paper cups. Allow to cool completely before serving.

Coconut Almond BALLS

4 cups flaked coconut
¼ cup light corn syrup
¼ cup shortening

1 (12-ounce) package
    semisweet chocolate chips
26 whole almonds

Line two cookie sheets with waxed paper and place large cooling rack on top. Place the coconut in large bowl. Heat the corn syrup for 1 minute in the microwave or until syrup boils. Pour syrup immediately over coconut and stir until well mixed. Shape coconut into 26 balls and place on wire racks. Allow to set for 10 minutes, and then reroll each ball to keep loose ends from sticking out. Melt the shortening and chocolate chips together in large glass bowl in the microwave. Working quickly, spoon 1 tablespoon of the chocolate mixture over each ball. Lightly press an almond on top of each ball. Let stand until balls are set.

Cherry SURPRISES

½ cup butter, softened
1¾ cups powdered sugar
1 teaspoon orange juice

1½ cups shredded coconut
1 (10-ounce) jar stemless
    maraschino cherries, drained

In a medium bowl, combine butter, powdered sugar, and orange juice. Stir in the coconut and mix until well combined. Wrap coconut mixture around each cherry to cover completely. Store in an airtight container in the refrigerator until ready to serve.

Cherry NUT BALLS

1 cup butter, softened
1 cup powdered sugar
1 teaspoon vanilla
½ cup maraschino cherries, chopped

¾ cup coconut
2 cups uncooked oats
Finely ground nuts to roll balls in

Beat the butter, sugar, vanilla, cherries, and coconut in a large bowl. Mix in the oats. Cover, and refrigerate for 3 hours. Shape the mixture into 1-inch balls. Roll each ball in the chopped nuts. Store in an airtight container.

Cream Cheese MINTS

1 (3-ounce) package
   cream cheese, softened
1 tablespoon butter, softened
3 cups powdered sugar

2 drops peppermint oil
Any color food coloring
   (optional)

In a large bowl, combine cream cheese, butter, and powdered sugar. Stir in peppermint oil. Color as desired with food coloring or leave white. Roll the cream cheese mixture into small balls, and place on a sheet of waxed paper. Flatten with a fork dipped in powdered sugar. Let dry for about 2 hours on waxed paper, then freeze or refrigerate.

Coconut FROGS

½ cup cocoa
2 cups sugar
½ cup milk
½ cup butter

1 teaspoon vanilla extract
1 cup flaked coconut
3 cups quick-cooking oats

Line two cookie sheets with waxed paper; set aside. In a large saucepan, stir together cocoa, sugar, milk, and butter. Boil for 5 minutes; remove from heat. Stir in vanilla, coconut, and oats. Mix well. Drop by tablespoonfuls onto the prepared cookie sheets. Refrigerate for 1 hour or until set. Store in the refrigerator.

Martha Washington CANDIES

1 cup margarine
4 cups powdered sugar
1 (14-ounce) can sweetened
   condensed milk

2 cups shredded coconut
2 cups chopped pecans
2 teaspoons vanilla extract
2 cups semisweet chocolate chips

Line two cookie sheets with waxed paper; set aside. In a large bowl, combine margarine, powdered sugar, and sweetened condensed milk; mix well. Add coconut, pecans, and vanilla. Mix until well combined. Chill until firm enough to handle. Form mixture into small balls and place on prepared cookie sheets. Chill until completely firm. Melt chocolate chips in a saucepan. Using a toothpick, dip the balls into the melted chocolate. Allow to cool on waxed paper.

Chocolate-Covered PRETZELS

1 cup semisweet chocolate chips
1 cup white chocolate chips,
    divided

1½ tablespoons shortening,
    divided
25 small pretzels

Cover a cookie sheet with waxed paper. Combine chocolate chips, $^2/_3$ cup white chocolate chips, and 1 tablespoon shortening in a large microwave-safe bowl. Microwave on high (100%) for 1 minute; stir. Microwave on high an additional 1–1$^1/_2$ minutes until chips are melted when stirred. Dip each pretzel into the mixture, and place on the prepared cookie sheet. Combine the remaining $^1/_3$ cup white chocolate chips and the $^1/_2$ teaspoon shortening in a small microwave-safe bowl. Microwave on high for 20–30 seconds; stir. Using a toothpick, drizzle the mixture across the pretzels. Refrigerate until set. Store in an airtight container.

Crispy PEANUT BUTTER BARS

½ stick butter or margarine
1 (10-ounce) bag miniature
   marshmallows

2 tablespoons peanut butter
6 cups crispy rice cereal

Grease a 9x13-inch pan; set aside. In a large microwave-safe bowl, combine the butter and marshmallows. Microwave on high (100%) for 3 minutes. Stir well. Add peanut butter and stir until well blended. Add rice cereal. Stir until evenly coated. Pour mixture into prepared pan. Let stand for 10 minutes. Cut into squares.

Chewy CHOCOLATE BARS

¾ cup honey
1 cup peanut butter
1 cup semisweet chocolate chips

1½ cups miniature marshmallows
3 cups crispy rice cereal
1 cup salted peanuts

In a large saucepan over medium heat, melt the honey and peanut butter. Bring to a boil. Stir in chocolate chips and marshmallows. Stir until smooth. Add the cereal and peanuts. Blend well and remove from heat. Pour into a lightly greased 9x13-inch pan. Press firmly with a spatula. Let stand for 10 minutes. Cut into bars before hardening.

Microwave TOFFEE

½ cup chopped pecans
½ cup (1 stick) butter
1 cup sugar
1 teaspoon salt

¼ cup water
½ cup semisweet chocolate chips
¼ cup chopped pecans

Sprinkle ½ cup pecans in a 9-inch circle on a greased cookie sheet and set aside. Coat the top 2 inches of a 2-quart measuring cup with butter. Add butter, sugar, salt, and water; do not stir. Microwave on high (100%) for 10–11 minutes or until the mixture begins to turn light brown. Pour the mixture over the circle of pecans. Sprinkle with chocolate chips and let set for 1 minute. Spread the melted chips over toffee with knife and sprinkle with ¼ cup pecans. Chill until firm. Break into bite-sized pieces. Store in an airtight container.

Pumpkin FUDGE

3 cups sugar
³/₄ cup butter
²/₃ cup evaporated milk
¹/₂ cup canned pumpkin
¹/₂ teaspoon ground cinnamon
¹/₄ teaspoon ground ginger

¹/₄ teaspoon ground nutmeg
1 (12-ounce) package
   butterscotch chips
1 (7-ounce) jar marshmallow crème
1 cup chopped pecans
1 teaspoon vanilla extract

Grease a 9x13-inch baking pan. In a large saucepan, combine the sugar, butter, evaporated milk, pumpkin, cinnamon, ginger, and nutmeg. Bring the mixture to a boil, stirring constantly. Reduce heat. Boil over medium heat until mixture registers 234 degrees on a candy thermometer (about 25 minutes), stirring constantly. Remove from the heat and stir in the butterscotch chips until completely melted. Add the marshmallow crème, pecans, and vanilla. Mix until combined. Pour the mixture into the prepared pan. Spread evenly. Allow to cool at room temperature. Cut into squares and wrap tightly in plastic wrap. Store in the refrigerator.

Chocolate Butterscotch FUDGE

1 cup butterscotch chips
1 (14-ounce) can sweetened
    condensed milk
2 cups (12-ounce package)
    semisweet chocolate chips

1 teaspoon vanilla extract
½ cup chopped walnuts

Line an 8-inch square pan with aluminum foil. Combine butterscotch chips and ⅓ cup sweetened condensed milk in a small microwave-safe bowl; set aside. Place chocolate chips, the remaining sweetened condensed milk, and vanilla in a medium, microwave-safe bowl. Microwave on high (100%) for 1 minute. Stir until the chips are completely melted. Stir in the walnuts. Spread evenly into the prepared pan. Microwave butterscotch chip mixture on high for 45 seconds. Stir until chips are completely melted. Spread evenly over the chocolate layer. Refrigerate until firm. Remove from the pan, and peel off the foil. Place on a cutting board and cut into squares. Store in an airtight container in the refrigerator.

Festive FUDGE CUTOUTS

3 cups (1½ 12-ounce packages)
   semisweet chocolate chips
1 (14-ounce) can sweetened
   condensed milk

⅛ teaspoon salt
1½ teaspoons vanilla extract

Line a 9x13-inch pan with aluminum foil, extending the foil over the edges of the pan. Place chocolate chips, sweetened condensed milk, and salt in a large microwave-safe bowl. Microwave on high (100%) for 1 minute; stir. Microwave on high for an additional 20–30 seconds until chips are melted and smooth when stirred. Stir in the vanilla. Pour mixture into the prepared pan. Cover, and refrigerate until firm. Use the foil to lift the fudge out of the pan. Peel off foil and place onto a cutting board. Using holiday cookie cutters, cut fudge into festive shapes. Store in an airtight container.

Variations
Use the following instead of chocolate chips for a variety of fudge flavors:
PEANUT BUTTER FUDGE: Substitute $2\frac{1}{2}$ cups peanut butter chips.
WHITE CHOCOLATE FUDGE: Substitute $3\frac{1}{2}$ cups white chocolate chips.

Potato CANDY

¼ cup cooked white potatoes
1 teaspoon vanilla extract

1 box powdered sugar
Peanut butter

Mash potatoes. Add the vanilla and approximately 1 box of powdered sugar until a soft dough is formed. Divide dough into fourths. Roll each piece of dough between waxed paper until ⅛ inch thick. Spread a thin layer of peanut butter on each layer. Roll up like a jelly roll. Refrigerate overnight. Cut into slices. Sprinkle with powdered sugar if desired.

Candy Cane BARK

8 ounces white chocolate   4 tablespoons candy canes, crushed
8 ounces dark chocolate

Place the white and dark chocolate in a microwave-safe bowl. Microwave on high (100%) for 30 seconds; stir. Continue microwaving at 30-second intervals until smooth when stirred. Add in crushed candy canes. Pour the mixture onto a cookie sheet in a thin layer. Freeze for up to 30 minutes. Break into small pieces.

Cookie BARK

1 (20-ounce) package chocolate
  sandwich cookies with
  cream filling

2 (18½-ounce) packages
  white chocolate

Line a 15x10x1-inch jelly-roll pan with waxed paper. Coat paper with a non-stick cooking spray; set aside. Break half of the cookies into coarse pieces and place in a large bowl. In a microwave-safe bowl, melt one package of the white chocolate in the microwave. Quickly fold melted chocolate into the broken cookie pieces. Pour the mixture into the prepared pan and spread to cover half of the pan. Repeat the process with the remaining chocolate and cookies. Refrigerate until solid. Remove from the pan and carefully peel off the waxed paper. Place bark on a large cutting board and cut into pieces with a large knife. Store in an airtight container.

Cheery Cherry CHRISTMAS FUDGE

1 (8-ounce) can almond paste
1 (14-ounce) can sweetened condensed
   milk, divided
Red food coloring

1³/₄ cups semisweet
   chocolate chips
Red candied cherry halves
Sliced almonds

Line an 8-inch square pan with aluminum foil, extending the foil over the edges of the pan. Beat almond paste and ¼ cup sweetened condensed milk in a small bowl until it is well mixed. Add food coloring and beat until blended. Refrigerate for about 1 hour or until firm. Spread onto the bottom of prepared pan. Place chocolate chips and the remaining sweetened condensed milk in a medium microwave-safe bowl. Microwave on high (100%) for 1–1½ minutes or until chocolate is melted and smooth. Spread over top of the almond paste layer. Cover, and refrigerate until firm. Use the edges of the foil to lift out of the pan. Peel off the foil and cut fudge into squares. Garnish with cherry halves and sliced almonds. Store in an airtight container in the refrigerator.

Holiday PEANUT BUTTER CHOCOLATE FUDGE

3 cups (1½ packages) semisweet
   chocolate chips
1 (14-ounce) can sweetened
   condensed milk
Dash salt
½ cup chopped nuts (optional)

1½ teaspoons vanilla extract
1⅔ cups (10-ounce package)
   peanut butter chips, divided
½ cup whipping cream

Line an 8-inch square pan with waxed paper. Melt chocolate chips and sweetened condensed milk in a medium saucepan over low heat, stirring constantly. Stir in salt. Remove from heat. Stir in nuts, if desired, vanilla, and ⅔ cup peanut butter chips. Pour into prepared pan and spread evenly with a spatula. Melt the remaining peanut butter chips with the whipping cream over low heat, stirring constantly, until smooth and thick. Spread over chocolate. Refrigerate until firm. Turn the fudge onto a cutting board and peel off the waxed paper. Cut the fudge into squares. Store in an airtight container in the refrigerator.

Mocha FUDGE

2 cups (12-ounce package) semisweet chocolate chips
1 cup milk chocolate chips
2 tablespoons milk
1 (14-ounce) can sweetened condensed milk

4 teaspoons powdered instant coffee dissolved in
1 tablespoon warm water
1 tablespoon vanilla extract
1 cup chopped nuts

Line an 8-inch square pan with aluminum foil. Combine both kinds of chips, milk, sweetened condensed milk, coffee, and vanilla in a medium saucepan. Cook over low heat until chips are melted, stirring constantly. Remove from the heat and stir in nuts. Pour into the prepared pan and spread evenly with a spatula. Refrigerate until firm. Remove from the pan and peel off foil. Place onto a cutting board and cut into squares. Store in an airtight container in the refrigerator.

Pineapple FUDGE

1 cup evaporated milk
3 cups sugar
2 tablespoons butter

1 cup crushed pineapple, drained
2 teaspoons lemon juice

Grease a 9-inch square pan; set aside. In a saucepan, combine evaporated milk, sugar, and butter. Heat to boiling. Stir in pineapple and heat to soft-ball stage (236 degrees), stirring constantly for about 25 minutes. Remove from heat and allow to cool. Stir in lemon juice and beat until mixture is smooth. Pour into the prepared pan. Allow to cool completely before cutting into squares.

Ice Cream FUDGE

2 pounds semisweet chocolate,
    chopped
1 pint mint ice cream, slightly
    thawed

1 cup chopped pecans

Line a 9-inch square pan with aluminum foil. Lightly grease the foil. Place the chocolate in a large microwave-safe bowl. Microwave on high (100%) for 1 minute and 45 seconds; stir. Add the thawed ice cream and beat until smooth. Stir in the pecans. Pour into the prepared pan. Refrigerate until fudge is firm. Cut into squares and store in an airtight container in the refrigerator.

Peanut Butter CHOCOLATE CHIP FUDGE

1 ½ cups sugar
⅔ cup (5-ounce can) evaporated milk
2 tablespoons butter
1 ½ cups miniature marshmallows

1 ¾ cups (11-ounce package)
   peanut butter and milk
   chocolate chips
1 teaspoon vanilla extract

Line an 8-inch square baking pan with aluminum foil. Grease foil with butter and set aside. Combine the sugar, evaporated milk, and butter in a large saucepan. Cook over medium heat, stirring constantly. Bring to a rolling boil. Boil, stirring constantly for 5 minutes. Remove from heat and stir in the marshmallows, chips, and vanilla. Continue stirring until marshmallows are completely melted. Pour mixture into prepared pan. Refrigerate for 1 hour or until firm. Cut fudge into squares. Store in an airtight container in a cool, dry place.

German CHOCOLATE FUDGE

2 cups semisweet chocolate chips
12 (1-ounce) squares German
   sweet chocolate
1 (7-ounce) jar marshmallow crème
4½ cups sugar

2 tablespoons butter
1 (12-ounce) can evaporated milk
⅛ teaspoon salt
2 cups chopped pecans

Grease a 15x10x1-inch pan; set aside. Combine chocolate chips, German sweet chocolate, and marshmallow crème in large bowl; set aside. Combine sugar, butter, evaporated milk, and salt in a heavy skillet. Bring to a boil over medium heat. Cook for 6 minutes, stirring constantly. Pour hot syrup over the chocolate mixture. Stir until smooth. Stir in pecans. Pour mixture into the prepared pan. Let stand until firm; cut into squares.

Come to Bethlehem and see
Him whose birth the angels sing;
Come adore on bended knee
Christ the Lord, the newborn King.

TRADITIONAL FRENCH CAROL

Sweet Christmas Treats

Now that the time has come wherein
Our Savior Christ was born,
The larder's full of beef and pork,
The granary's full of corn.
As God hath plenty to thee sent,
Take comfort of thy labors,
And let it never thee repent
To feed thy needy neighbors.

AUTHOR UNKNOWN

Cherry CHRISTMAS DESSERT

1 (21-ounce) can cherry pie filling
1 (8-ounce) container whipped cream
1 (14-ounce) can sweetened
  condensed milk

1 (10-ounce) can crushed
  pineapple, drained
1 package cherry gelatin mix, dry
1/2 cup chopped nuts

Combine all ingredients above in a large bowl; mix well. Refrigerate for at least 4 hours before serving.

Chocolate MOUSSE

1 envelope gelatin (unflavored)
1/4 cup sugar
1 cup semisweet chocolate chips
4 eggs, separated

1/4 teaspoon salt
1/3 cup sugar
2 cups whipping cream
2 toffee candy bars, chopped
Chocolate wafers

In a medium saucepan, add ¼ cup of water. Dissolve the gelatin and ¼ cup sugar in the water over low heat. Stir in the chocolate chips until melted. Remove from the heat and beat in the egg yolks one at a time. Cool in a covered bowl for 10–15 minutes. In a separate bowl, add egg whites and salt. Beat until mixture has soft peaks. Beat ⅓ cup of sugar into the egg whites. Carefully fold the egg whites into the chocolate mixture. In a separate bowl, add the whipping cream and whip until it becomes thicker and is creating soft peaks. Fold half of the whipped cream into the chocolate mixture. Place a large spoonful of mousse in a parfait glass, followed by a spoonful of candy and whipped cream. Repeat for each layer. Top with whipped cream and serve with chocolate wafers.

Chocolate Rainbow ROLLS

½ cup (1 stick) butter or margarine
2 cups (12-ounce package)
    semisweet chocolate chips

6 cups (10½-ounce package)
    miniature colored marshmallows
1 cup finely chopped nuts
Additional chopped nuts

In a medium saucepan, over low heat, melt the butter and the chocolate chips until blended, stirring constantly. Remove from heat and cool for 5 minutes. Stir in the marshmallows and 1 cup of nuts. Do not let the marshmallows melt. On a sheet of waxed paper, shape the mixture into two 7-inch rolls. Wrap the rolls in aluminum foil and refrigerate for about 20–25 minutes. To coat the rolls, roll them in the additional nuts. Wrap, and refrigerate overnight. Cut the rolls into ¼-inch slices. Store in an airtight container in a cool, dry place. Makes about 3 dozen slices.

Peppermint PRETZEL CANES

6 ounces vanilla flavor candy coating,
  cut into pieces
2 tablespoons shortening

2/3 cup peppermint candies,
  finely crushed
12 pretzel rods

Line a cookie sheet with waxed paper. Melt candy coating and shortening in a medium saucepan over low heat, stirring occasionally. Pour the mixture into a shallow baking pan; carefully set the baking dish in hot water to keep the coating soft. Sprinkle the crushed peppermint candy over a separate sheet of waxed paper. Roll the pretzels in the hot coating, allowing excess to drip off. Roll each coated pretzel in crushed candy. Place on lined cookie sheet and let stand until set.

Holiday DESSERT

1 (3.9-ounce) package pistachio
    instant pudding mix
1 (1-pound) can crushed pineapple

1 (8-ounce) container whipped cream
1 cup miniature marshmallows

In a large bowl, combine the pudding mix and the pineapple. Add whipped cream and marshmallows; stir well. Refrigerate for 1 hour before serving.

No-Bake Chocolate DESSERT

20 chocolate sandwich
   cookies, crushed
1 (8-ounce) package cream
   cheese, softened
2 cups powdered sugar

$3/4$ cup peanut butter
1 (12-ounce) container frozen
   whipped topping, thawed

Press the crushed cookies into the bottom of a 9x13-inch pan, reserving a few for decoration. In a medium bowl, combine the cream cheese and powdered sugar; beat well. Stir in the peanut butter until well blended. Fold in the whipped topping. Spread mixture over the crushed cookie layer. Sprinkle the reserved cookie pieces over top. Freeze for 1–2 hours. Allow to thaw 10–15 minutes before cutting and serving.

Cherry Cheese SQUARES

1 1/4 cups graham cracker crumbs
1/4 cup butter, melted
1 (8-ounce) package cream
  cheese, softened

1 cup powdered sugar
1/2 teaspoon vanilla extract
1 cup frozen whipped topping, thawed
1 (21-ounce) can cherry pie filling

Combine graham cracker crumbs and melted butter in an 8-inch square pan. Press into the bottom of the pan to form a crust. Chill in the refrigerator. In a large bowl, beat the cream cheese until fluffy; add the powdered sugar and vanilla; beat until smooth. Fold the whipped topping into the cream cheese mixture. Spread the mixture onto the chilled graham cracker crust and spoon cherry pie filling over it. Cover and place in the freezer. Before completely frozen, cut into small squares; return to the freezer. Remove from freezer 20–30 minutes before serving. Can be stored in the refrigerator.

No-Bake PEANUT CHOCOLATE BROWNIES

4 cups graham cracker crumbs
1 cup peanuts, chopped
½ cup powdered sugar
¼ cup peanut butter

2 cups semisweet chocolate chips
1 cup evaporated milk
1 teaspoon vanilla extract

Grease a 9-inch square pan; set aside. In a medium bowl, combine the graham cracker crumbs, peanuts, powdered sugar, and peanut butter with a pastry blender. In a small saucepan, over low heat, melt the chocolate chips with the evaporated milk, stirring constantly. Remove from heat and stir in the vanilla. Remove ½ cup of the melted chocolate mixture and set aside. Pour the remaining chocolate mixture over the graham cracker crumb mixture and stir until well blended. Spread evenly in the prepared pan. Frost with the reserved chocolate mixture. Chill in the refrigerator for at least 1 hour.

Cheesecake PUDDING

1 (8-ounce) package cream
    cheese, softened
1 stick butter
1 cup powdered sugar
2 (3.9-ounce) boxes instant
    vanilla pudding mix

3 cups milk
1 small container frozen
    whipped topping, thawed
3 cups chocolate sandwich
    cookies, crushed

In a large bowl, mix cream cheese, butter, and powdered sugar until well blended. In a separate bowl, combine pudding mix and milk; mix well. Add the whipped topping. Pour the pudding mixture into the cream cheese mixture and stir until completely blended. In parfait glasses, layer crushed cookies and pudding mixture, ending with the crushed cookies. Continue filling glasses until mixture is gone.

Pumpkin PARFAIT

1 can pumpkin puree
1 (3.9-ounce) package instant
  vanilla pudding mix
1 teaspoon pumpkin pie spice

1 cup evaporated milk
1 cup milk
Whipped topping (optional)

In a large mixing bowl, combine the pumpkin puree, vanilla pudding mix, pumpkin pie spice, evaporated milk, and milk. Stir until smooth. Place mixture in parfait glasses and chill until set. Top parfaits with whipped topping if desired.

No-Bake GRANOLA BARS

2 ½ cups crisp rice cereal
2 cups quick-cooking oats
½ cup raisins
½ cup brown sugar, firmly packed

½ cup light corn syrup
½ cup peanut butter
1 teaspoon vanilla extract
½ cup milk chocolate chips

In a large bowl, combine crisp rice cereal, oats, and raisins; set aside. In a small saucepan, over medium heat, bring the brown sugar and corn syrup to a boil, stirring constantly. Remove from heat and stir in peanut butter and vanilla until well blended. Pour the peanut butter mixture over the cereal mixture and toss until well coated. Let stand for 10 minutes. Stir in the chocolate chips. Press the mixture into a 9x13-inch pan. Allow to cool completely before cutting into bars.

Old-Fashioned CHRISTMAS PUDDING

2 cups fresh bread crumbs
¾ cup milk
2 eggs, well beaten
1 cup suet, finely chopped
½ teaspoon salt
1 cup brown sugar
1 cup flour
¼ teaspoon allspice
¼ teaspoon nutmeg
1 teaspoon cinnamon

1 teaspoon baking powder
¼ teaspoon baking soda
1 cup raisins
1 cup orange peel
½ cup dates and cherries, chopped
1 apple, peeled
1 cup chopped walnuts
½ cup dark molasses
1 teaspoon lemon peel

In a large bowl, combine bread crumbs with milk, and let soak until moist. Add beaten eggs, chopped suet, salt, brown sugar, and flour. Add spices and all other ingredients, and mix well. Divide into two round balls. Tie in cheesecloth. Place a metal cookie cutter into a cooking pan. Pour in water to measure 1½ inches. Set pudding on top of cookie cutter. Cover pan and heat water to boiling over high heat. Reduce heat to low and simmer pudding until toothpick inserted through cheesecloth comes out clean. Serve warm with hard sauce.

Hard Sauce:

2 cups sugar   2 cups water

Cook and thicken with cornstarch. Add dash of salt to taste. Serve warm over Old-Fashioned Christmas Pudding.

Christmas CANDY BARS

1 cup sugar	6 cups rice flakes cereal
1 cup light corn syrup	6 ounces milk chocolate chips
1½ cups creamy peanut butter	6 ounces butterscotch chips

Grease a 9x13-inch pan; set aside. In a medium saucepan, bring sugar and corn syrup to a boil. Stir in the peanut butter; batter will be stiff. Mix in the cereal. Press into prepared pan. In a small microwave-safe bowl, add chocolate chips and butterscotch chips. Microwave on high (100%) at 15-second intervals until completely melted. Spread over the cereal mixture. Allow to set at room temperature until cool. Cut into bars.

Easy GRAHAM CRACKER TREATS

½ cup miniature chocolate chips
2 cups frozen whipped topping,
    thawed

⅔ cup miniature marshmallows
1 box of graham crackers

In a large mixing bowl, combine the first three ingredients. Mix well. Spoon the mixture onto one side of a graham cracker square. Use another square to cover the mixture. Continue making the graham cracker sandwiches until all of the marshmallow mixture is gone. Freeze sandwiches for 1 to 2 hours or until frozen. Serve frozen.

Christmas DESSERT PUDDING

4 (14-ounce) cans sweetened
   condensed milk
4 pints heavy whipping cream

1 (4-ounce) jar maraschino cherries
1 cup chopped almonds

Remove the labels from the cans of sweetened condensed milk and put them unopened into a large pot of gently boiling water. Allow to boil for about 3 hours. Make sure the water doesn't boil away. After 3 hours, take the cans out and chill in the refrigerator. When chilled, open the cans and put the contents into a large bowl. In a medium bowl, beat the whipping cream until thick, and fold into the bowl of sweetened condensed milk. Stir in the cherries and almonds.

What can I give Him,
Poor as I am?
If I were a shepherd,
I would bring Him a lamb.
If I were a Wise Man,
I would do my part.
Yet what can I give Him?
I give Him my heart.

CHRISTINA ROSSETTI

Holiday Party Mixes

Unless we make Christmas an occasion to share our blessings,

all the snow in Alaska won't make it "white."

BING CROSBY

I will honor Christmas in my heart, and try to keep it all the year.

CHARLES DICKENS

S'more MIX

2 cups honey or cinnamon
   graham cereal
1 cup salted peanuts

1 cup miniature marshmallows
½ cup milk chocolate chips
½ cup raisins

Combine all ingredients in a large, festive bowl.

Puppy CHOW

9 cups rice squares cereal
1/4 cup butter or margarine
1 cup semisweet chocolate chips

1/2 cup peanut butter
1 teaspoon vanilla extract
1 1/2 cups powdered sugar

Pour cereal into a large bowl; set aside. In a small microwave-safe bowl, combine butter, chocolate chips, and peanut butter. Microwave on high (100%) for 1–2 minutes or until chips are completely melted and smooth when stirred. Stir in vanilla. Pour mixture over the cereal. Pour half of the powdered sugar into a large sealable plastic bag. Add half of the cereal mixture into the bag and seal the top completely. Shake until the cereal is evenly coated with the powdered sugar. Pour the cereal onto a sheet of waxed paper. Pour the remaining powdered sugar into the bag, along with the remaining cereal mixture. Seal the opening and shake until coated. Pour onto the sheet of waxed paper and allow to cool completely. Store in an airtight container in a cool, dry place.

Cashew CRUNCH

2 cups milk chocolate chips
¾ cup chopped cashews
¾ cup chopped macadamia nuts

½ cup (1 stick) butter, softened
½ cup sugar
2 tablespoons light corn syrup

Line a 9-inch square pan with aluminum foil, extending the foil over the edges of the pan. Butter the foil. Cover the bottom of the pan with chocolate chips. Combine the cashews, macadamia nuts, butter, sugar, and corn syrup in a large skillet. Cook over low heat. Stir constantly until the butter is melted and the sugar is dissolved. Increase the heat to medium. Stir constantly until the mixture begins to cling together and turns brown. Pour the mixture over the chocolate chips. Cool until firm. Remove from the pan, and peel off the foil. Break into pieces. Store in an airtight container in a cool, dry place. Makes about ½ pound.

White Chocolate CHERRY CRUNCH

2 cups corn squares cereal
2 cups miniature pretzels
2 cups dry-roasted peanuts
1 cup miniature marshmallows
1 (3-ounce) package dried cherries

1 (12-ounce) package white
    chocolate chips
¼ cup half-and-half
¼ teaspoon almond extract

In a large bowl, combine the cereal, pretzels, peanuts, marshmallows, and cherries; set aside. In a large saucepan, over low heat, cook chocolate chips and half-and-half, stirring constantly until chips are melted. Stir in the almond extract. Pour the melted mixture over the dry ingredients. Toss gently until the dry ingredients are evenly coated. Drop the mixture by spoonfuls onto a sheet of waxed paper. Let stand about 1 hour or until set. Store loosely covered up to one week.

Vanilla PARTY MIX

1 (10-ounce) package miniature
    pretzels
5 cups rice squares cereal
1 (1-pound) package candy-
    coated chocolate pieces

2 (12-ounce) packages
    vanilla chips
3 tablespoons vegetable oil

In a large bowl, combine pretzels, cereal, and chocolate pieces; set aside. In a small, microwave-safe bowl, combine chips and vegetable oil. Microwave on high (100%) for 2 minutes. Stir, and microwave at high for 10 more seconds. Stir until smooth. Pour over cereal mixture and mix well. Spread onto waxed paper and allow to cool completely. Store in an airtight container in a cool, dry place.

Christmas PARTY MIX

1 (16-ounce) jar dry-roasted peanuts
1 (14-ounce) package chocolate-
    covered peanuts
1 (7-ounce) jar wheat nuts

2 (14-ounce) packages red and
    green candy-coated
    chocolate pieces

In a large bowl, combine all the ingredients. Stir well. Serve in a large festive bowl, or put in decorative glass jars to give as gifts.

Butterscotch PARTY MIX

2 cups rice squares cereal
2 cups small pretzel twists
1 cup dry-roasted peanuts

1 cup caramels, unwrapped,
   coarsely chopped
1 (11-ounce) package
   butterscotch chips

Coat a 9x13-inch baking pan with nonstick cooking spray. In a large bowl, combine cereal, pretzels, peanuts, and caramels. Place butterscotch chips in a medium microwave-safe bowl. Microwave at medium-high (70%) for 1 minute; stir. Microwave at 20-second intervals, stirring until smooth. Pour over the cereal mixture. Stir until evenly coated. Spread mixture into the prepared baking pan and let stand for 30 minutes or until firm. Break into small pieces.

Sweet PRETZEL MIX

2 cups pretzels, crushed

¼ cup salted peanuts

⅔ cup sweetened condensed milk

½ cup semisweet chocolate chips

½ cup butterscotch chips

¼ teaspoon vanilla extract

In a large mixing bowl, combine the crushed pretzels and peanuts; set aside. In a medium saucepan, combine the sweetened condensed milk, chocolate chips, and butterscotch chips. Cook over low heat, stirring constantly, until the chips are melted and smooth. Remove from heat and stir in vanilla. Pour the melted chip mixture over the pretzel mixture and toss to coat evenly. Drop by rounded spoonfuls onto a sheet of waxed paper. Allow to cool until firm. Store in an airtight container in a cool, dry place.

White Chocolate CHRISTMAS MIX

2 pounds white chocolate
3 cups toasted oat cereal
2 cups cashews

6 cups crispy rice squares cereal
2 cups thin pretzel sticks
1 (12-ounce) package miniature
candy-coated chocolate pieces

Melt white chocolate in a large saucepan over low heat or in microwave just until soft. Stir until completely melted. Combine all the other ingredients in a large bowl. Pour melted white chocolate over mixture; stir until evenly coated. Turn out onto waxed paper. Allow to cool. Break into pieces.

Macadamia CLUSTERS

8 ounces vanilla chips
2 (3½-ounce) packages
  macadamia nuts

½ tablespoon orange zest

Place the vanilla chips in a microwave-safe bowl. Microwave uncovered on high (100%) for 40–60 seconds. Stir until melted and smooth. Stir in nuts and orange zest. Drop mixture by teaspoonfuls onto a sheet of waxed paper. Allow to cool until set. Store in an airtight container in a cool, dry place.

And there were in the same country
shepherds abiding in the field,
keeping watch over their flock by night.
And, lo, the angel of the Lord came upon them,
and the glory of the Lord shone round about them:
and they were sore afraid. And the angel said unto them,
Fear not: for, behold, I bring you good tidings of great joy,
which shall be to all people.

Luke 2:8–10